Waiting For the Sleeping Beauty

Priya Singh

Ukiyoto Publishing

All global publishing rights are held by

Ukiyoto Publishing

Published in 2025

Content Copyright © Priya Singh

ISBN 9789370091085

All rights reserved.
No part of this publication may be reproduced, transmitted, or stored in a retrieval system, in any form by any means, electronic, mechanical, photocopying, recording or otherwise, without the prior permission of the publisher.

The moral rights of the author have been asserted.

This is a work of fiction. Names, characters, businesses, places, events, locales, and incidents are either the products of the author's imagination or used in a fictitious manner. Any resemblance to actual persons, living or dead, or actual events is purely coincidental.

This book is sold subject to the condition that it shall not by way of trade or otherwise, be lent, resold, hired out or otherwise circulated, without the publisher's prior consent, in any form of binding or cover other than that in which it is published.

www.ukiyoto.com

I dedicate this book "Waiting for the sleeping Beauty" to lord krishna & all my dearest readers .

Thanks
Priya Poetess

CONTENTS

Poem - 1 - Garden of Paradise	1
Poem - 2 - The wonderful garden	2
Poem - 3 - Feeling beautiful	3
Poem - 4 - Curiosity's call	4
Poem – 5 - Sunday's Plea	5
Poem – 6 - A feel of Joy	7
Poem - 7 - "Waiting for the Sleeping Beauty"	8
Poem – 8 - I Can't Sleep	9
Poem – 9 - Dreams of Meeting You	10
Poem - 10 - The Sweet Dream	11
Poem -11 - On the Way to the Garden	12
Poem -12 - The wait continues	13
Poem – 13 - The Garden's Radiance	14
Poem -14 - The Mysterious Guest	16
Poem -15 - The Guest Revealed	17
Poem -16 - In Her Dreams	18
Poem - 17 - Lost in Her Thoughts	19
Poem -18 - She's an Emotional Queen	20

Poem – 19 - Once Again in Her Garden	21
Poem - 20 - Finally Our Eyes Met	23
Poem -21 - First Conversation	24
Poem -22 - Sweet Memory	25
Poem -23 - Three Months Passed Away	26
Poem – 24 - The Sweetest Call	27
Poem – 25 - Deep Feelings	29
Poem – 26 - Composition in Garden	30
Poem – 27 - Pure Feelings	31
Poem - 28 - I Feel You	32
Poem - 29 - Asking Questions from Myself	33
Poem – 30 - Meeting with Him	34
Poem – 31 - I get touched	35
Poem - 32 - A Soul So Pure	36
Poem – 33 - Her phone call	37
Poem – 34 - Across the Distance	38
Poem – 35 - She Called Again	39
Poem – 36 - She confessed her heart	40
Poem - 37 - Time Flew Away	42
Poem – 38 - I Missed Him Suddenly	43

Poem – 39 - Funny Conversation	44
Poem - 40 - I Am Trying to Be Disciplined	46
Poem – 41 - His Words Heal Me	47
Poem - 42 - Success at Exam	48
Poem - 43 - The Most Beautiful Moment	49
Poem – 44 - Two Years Gone	50
Poem – 45 - I Got the Booker Prize	51
Poem – 46 - After Six Months	52
Poem – 47 - I Sang for Him	53
Poem – 48 - You Are Saved in My Eyes	54
Poem – 49 - Don't You Feel It's Tough to Love You	55
Poem – 50 - The Soulful Kiss	56
About the Author	*58*

Poem - 1 - Garden of Paradise

I stand here, morning's golden light
Unfolds, and I wonder, whose delight
Is this rose-berry garden, shining bright?
It's like a fantasy world, a wondrous sight
Beautiful birds flit, sing, and play
As if the queen herself might stroll this way
The air is filled with perfume's sweet scent
This garden's beauty leaves me lost, intent
A stranger might gaze, entranced, and stare
At this paradise, beyond compare
A gorgeous girl, with beauty to share
Lives hidden here, with secrets to spare
Guards wander, vigilant, and strong
Protection thundering, all day long
Secrecy surrounds, a mysterious veil
I'll have to peek, to unveil.

Poem - 2 - The wonderful garden

I am in a dilemma, for I've seen a garden so fair,

Perhaps it was the garden of the fairy queen, beyond compare.

The roses shine so hard, so hard, so hard,

The butterfly chatters with lovely birds.

The money plant dances in a fanciful way,

Marigold wants something to say.

They converse in fantasy, in their own sweet way,

Bathed in sunshine rays.

I am mesmerized by the garden's beauty rare,

The fragrance of the mango orchard is fruity and fair.

It seems something special is hidden here,

But I dare not step inside this royal castle, my heart does fear.

The servants and guards are vigilant and tight,

It seems the queen is resting inside, a peaceful sight.

Poem - 3 - Feeling beautiful

Today, I shall inquire about the garden's owner,

My thoughts are consumed by its beauty, I confess.

The oaks and vines haunt me still,

A place where I could spend my lifetime, entranced.

I approach the guard, with questions in mind.

"Excuse me, please come here," I say, polite and kind.

"Yeah, gentlemen, how may I assist you?" he replies.

I ask, with curiosity, "To whom does this garden belong?"

The guard responds, "You're new here, in Shylock's city, I see.

This garden's expensive, its ticket price a luxury.

It belongs to Poetess Love, the queen of dreams, so divine."

"In daylight, she weaves poetic verse, and at night, she dreams,"

The guard continues, "This garden is her sanctuary, where creativity beams."

"I can disclose no more," he says, with a hint of secrecy.

"Please leave, gentlemen. Without a purpose, you can't roam carefree.

This garden is special, and I must ensure its safety.

Poem - 4 - Curiosity's call

My curiosity grows, and I confess,

That garden amazes me, and I'm drawn to its finesse.

I yearn to return, to experience its charm anew,

The guards revealed it's the poet's sanctuary, where creativity shines through.

That garden is indeed full of elegance and poise,

I long to see the Poetess, whose face I've yet to disclose.

But the guard bars my entry, and I'm left to ponder and plan,

How to gain access, and meet the poet, if I can.

Poem – 5 - Sunday's Plea

It's Sunday time once more,

I've returned to this enchanting garden's door.

If the guards see me again, I fear,

I'll struggle to seek pardon, my anxiety clear.

I stand by the roadside, hesitant and still,

When suddenly I hear a familiar voice's chill.

"Oh, it's the security guard once more," I sigh.

"Hello, excuse me, you've returned, I see you're back to try."

"You know I told you yesterday," the guard begins,

"This garden's private, not a place for casual visits or kin."

I plead, "I'm just a gentle soul, I mean no harm,

I yearn to bask in this warm sunshine, dispel my alarm."

"Tomorrow's my UPSC exam, I seek refuge from stress,

Your garden's fragrance is refreshing, a tranquil caress."

The guard's expression softens, yet he remains firm,

"Gentle boy, please understand, this garden's the poetess's private term."

"It's her residence, her comfort zone, where she resides,

I request you to visit elsewhere, other gardens where you can abide.

There are many beautiful spaces to ease your exam-day fears,

Please respect the poetess's privacy, and calm your doubts through cheers."

Poem – 6 - A feel of Joy

I try to convince the guard, "Oh God, you're not understanding,

It's okay, my friend, let me feel the garden's breeze by standing here."

The guard's expression softens, and he says, "Listen, gentle boy,

You may come inside, but remember, don't cross the red border line."

"You can sit in the corner swing," he adds with a gentle tone,

I thank him, curious, "Why the change of heart? Fifteen minutes ago, you were strict and stern."

The guard smiles, "You seem like a gentle soul, preparing for a tough exam,

I thought to help you in a humanistic way." He pauses, "But remember, you must leave before 12:00 noon."

Poem - 7 - "Waiting for the Sleeping Beauty"

"May I know, sir, what happens after 12 noon?"

I ask the guard, curious about the poetess's routine.

"Miss Poetess will come to her garden to compose and study,"

he replies, "She finds inspiration in the garden's beauty."

I ask, "So, what is she doing right now?"

The guard smiles, "She sleeps till 11:00 am, her morning starts late."

"In winter, she comes to the garden after 12:00 noon,"

he adds, "Here, she composes, rests, and finds her peaceful nest."

"This garden is her paradise," he says with a gentle tone.

I thank him for the information and decide to rest,

"As I have to leave before 12:00 noon," I say, closing my eyes, at peace.

Poem – 8 - I Can't Sleep

My plan worked, I'm happy and thrilled,

The exam excuse let me enter, my heart fulfilled.

But now I yearn to see the sleeping beauty rare,

The gorgeous poetess, who sleeps till noon's warm air.

I long to see her, to wish her good morning at noon,

Though I'm unsure if fate will grant me this sweet boon.

Today I've entered the garden, perhaps someday she'll appear,

Before 12:00, and my heart will skip a beat, my soul clear.

But if we meet, what words will I say?

I'm like a dreaming poet, lost in love's sweet way.

I've never met a poet before, with a heart so pure and bright,

What if she steals my heart, and I take flight?

Poem – 9 - Dreams of Meeting You

In slumber's realm, I see your face,
Poetess, enchantress of this secret place.
Your garden's beauty, a reflection of your soul,
A haven where creativity makes its goal.
I dream of strolling through the garden's gate,
Where roses bloom, and poetry creates.
I long to hear your voice, a melodic sound,
As you recite verses, with heart and soul unbound.
In this fantasy, I see us meet,
Under the oak tree, where sunlight softly greets.
We talk of poetry, of dreams and heart's desire,
Our conversation flows, like a gentle, sweet fire.
But dawn awakens, and the dream fades away,
Leaving me with longing, to meet you someday.
Perhaps fate will bring us together, in this garden fair,
And our love for poetry will be the bond we share.

Poem - 10 - The Sweet Dream

Oh God, what a sweet dream I've seen,

I didn't want it to end, but awake I've been.

It felt like a shock, a sudden, cruel fate,

To leave the world of dreams, where love and poetry wait.

I met the sleeping beauty, the poetess divine,

During my slumber, her voice and verse entwined.

Her recitation of poetry, a symphony so sweet,

Left me enchanted, my heart skipped a beat.

Oh God, I'm overwhelmed, my emotions in disarray,

Excitement and longing, in a tumultuous sway.

I wonder, will I fall for her, or her poetry's charm?

To win her heart, a daunting task, a challenge to disarm.

Poem -11 - On the Way to the Garden

The weather's chilled today, yet more beautiful than ever,

As I step through the garden gate, my heart starts to quiver.

I don't know where or when I'll catch a glimpse of her face,

The sleeping beauty, the poetess, in this sacred, secret place.

I sit amidst the blooms, lost in storybooks once more,

Imagining the poetess's looks, her beauty I adore.

But time ticks on, it's almost twelve noon, I must depart,

I feel like a thief, stealing moments, hiding in her heart.

I'll cherish this brief escape, this stolen moment in time,

And hold onto the hope of meeting her, sublime.

Poem -12 - The wait continues

Ten days have passed, and my daily visits seem in vain,

My enthusiasm wanes, as I wonder how much longer to sustain.

Should I return once more, or abandon my quest?

To meet the poetess, should I try or forget my unrest?

Oh God, I'm restless, yearning to see her face,

Why does she live in secrecy, a confidential, hidden place?

Perhaps she's proud and self-absorbed, avoiding strangers' gaze,

Yet, her garden remains my comfort zone, a soothing, peaceful daze.

Let me try once more, one last, fervent attempt,

To catch a glimpse of her, to finally meet my heart's intent.

Poem – 13 - The Garden's Radiance

Today, the garden shines with extraordinary delight,

Extremely decorated, a wondrous, autumnal sight.

I asked the guard, "What's the reason for this display?"

He smiled, "It's like paradise, even in autumn's gray."

As I glanced around, I caught a glimpse of her face,

But she turned away, ascending the stairs with gentle pace.

The beauty she carried was breath-taking, a treasure to behold,

Leaving me enchanted, my heart with wonder unfold.

The guard whispered, "Please leave soon, we have more to prepare,

Tomorrow, the poetess's dearest guest will arrive, beyond compare."

He added, "She woke up early, her sleepy nest forsaken,

Busy with preparations, her heart with joy unspoken."

I understood, "That's why the garden looks like paradise today."

The guard nodded, "Yes, the poetess checked the preparations thrice, in every way."

He smiled, "Tomorrow, she'll forego her noonday rest,

Eager to meet her special guest, and be at her best."

He bid me farewell, "Excuse us today, and tomorrow, too,

But after that, you're welcome to return, and study in our garden anew."

Poem -14 - The Mysterious Guest

Oh God, today I caught a glimpse of her face,

But my curiosity has grown, a nagging, restless pace.

Who is this special guest, this favourite person of hers?

The one who brings such joy, and stirs her heart with tender concerns?

The poetess is busy with preparations, her heart aglow,

I'm consumed by wonder, my mind in a whirl, don't know where to go.

Maybe it's her dream boy? No, no, that can't be,

Poets keep such secrets hidden, their hearts locked, you see.

Then who is this enigmatic guest, this mystery to unfold?

Tomorrow, I'll return, and perhaps, the truth will be told.

I'll see the poetess and her favourite person, face to face,

And maybe, just maybe, the secrets of her heart will find their place.

Poem -15 - The Guest Revealed

It's morning, I reach the garden gate,

Oh my God, the poetess stands with hundreds of roses in wait.

She's so beautiful, full of grace,

Waiting for her favourite person with a loving face.

She keeps checking her watch, then a big car arrives,

The poetess rushes, my heartbeat rises with surprise.

A famous person steps out, founder of Ojaank IAS Academy,

The poetess bows to touch his feet, he hugs her with glee.

She's overwhelmed, can't speak a word,

All her emotions merge in that hug, so unheard.

"My world's best teacher," she says with a smile,

He congratulates her on an international award, all the while.

He says, "I care for my poetic students too,"

The poetess invites him in, "Please come, no hurry, no time to pursue."

I'm amazed by her manners, her voice so sweet,

A true creator, a heart that beats with love, so unique.

Poem -16 - In Her Dreams

Oh my God, she's breathtakingly beautiful,

A perfect blend of beauty and intellect, a rare find, so true.

Her ethics and values, a testament to her noble soul,

The way she greeted her teacher, with respect, her heart's goal.

Her deep affection shines through, with tears that gently fall,

A beauty so gorgeous, yet soft, she stands tall.

Like ice that melts, my heart surrenders to her charm,

A rose holding a rose, her beauty disarms.

Emotional and deep, her heart beats with love and light,

In this manipulative world, how does she keep her spirit bright?

If someone breaks her heart, how will she survive the pain?

Yet, like the moon, she shines on, a constant, gentle glow that remains.

Poem - 17 - Lost in Her Thoughts

She's as lovely as a rose, radiant as the sun,

A beauty that enthralls, forever just begun.

Raindrops and snowflakes swirl, as I behold her sight,

Her sparkling eyes shine bright, her dusky white face alight.

Her gorgeous smile captivates, my heart skips a beat,

At first glance, she's my choice, my soul's sweet retreat.

She's a fairy, and her garden, my paradise found,

In her presence, I'm lost, forever enchanted, without a sound.

With every breath, I'm drawn to her lovely face,

My heart beats for her alone, in this wondrous, secret place.

Time stands still, as I gaze into her shining eyes,

My love for her forever grows, like a rose that never dies.

In her love, I find my home, my heart's sweet, peaceful nest.

Poem -18 - She's an Emotional Queen

She's an emotional queen, with a heart so divine,

In daylight, she dreams, with a soul so sublime.

Like an innocent queen, with a gentle, loving face,

She's a vision of beauty, in a tranquil, peaceful space.

In a dress of red roses, she's a wondrous sight,

Holding a bouquet of roses, with fingers adorned with diamond light.

Her eyes entwined, like a fairy tale come true,

I'm curious to know, the poetic verses she recites anew.

She and her garden, are beautiful, alike,

A haven of peace, where love and beauty take flight.

I'm drawn to her garden, like a magnet to its core,

Unable to resist, the allure of her beauty, forever more.

Poem – 19 - Once Again in Her Garden

With a smiling face, I entered the garden once more,

The guard welcomed me, and opened the gate as before.

I sat in my swing, with a few books by my side,

Wishing the poetess could hear my heart's gentle tide.

I yearned to talk to her, to meet her soon, to share,

My thoughts, my feelings, my love, my tender care.

I asked the guard, "Can I meet the poetess, please?"

He replied, "She won't meet strangers, only those she holds with ease."

"You're not a poet, nor her favourite person, I'm afraid,"

The guard said gently, "Please, just read your books, don't create a scene or shade."

"I've let you in the garden because you seem a gentle soul,"

He continued, "Don't try to meet her, it's not possible, I'm afraid, it's her rule."

The poetess is protected, guarded every single day,

She meets with no one, unless her father gives the say.

The guard's words were clear, "I'm sorry, I can't help you, my friend,"

He advised, "Prepare for your exams, and let your stress end."

Poem - 20 - Finally Our Eyes Met

I lay on the swing, books in hand,
My eyes closed, in a relaxed mood, so grand.
The air blew strong, and a paper flew by,
Landing on my face, catching my eye.
I took the paper, about to read the line,
When the poetess approached, her eyes divine.
Without a word, she took the paper from me,
Leaving me silent, standing, lost in her sea.
For a moment, our eyes met, pure and true,
A precious time, forever shining through.
Before she could ask, the rain started to pour,
She folded the paper, and tucked it in her coat once more.
She stepped into the shade, beckoning me near,
Pointing her finger, inviting me to come clear.
For me, it was paradise, the gates swung wide,
I held my book close, and stepped inside.
Her eyes questioned me, seeking to know my name,
And I, entranced by her beauty, felt no rain.

Poem -21 - First Conversation

We stood face to face in the garden shade,
Our first conversation, a gentle, sweet trade.
"I'm Vivansh," I said, entranced by her sight,
"Your garden's beauty mesmerizes me, day and night."
"I come here daily," I confessed, "to read and prepare,
For the UPSC exam, a challenge I must share."
She smiled, her eyes sparkling with kindness and light,
"It's alright, you're welcome here, day or night."
"This garden's my sanctuary," she said with a grin,
"For me and my dear friends, a peaceful haven within."
But you seem like a gentle soul, she added with a smile,
So please, come back daily, stay awhile."
I felt a connection, a sense of ease and peace,
As we sat together, firewoods warming the release.
She offered coffee or chocolate milk, a kind gesture true,
But I declined, thanking her, and bid adieu.
With a smile, I said goodbye, and left the garden shade,
Feeling grateful for the encounter, a memory to be made.
The warmth in her eyes, the innocence on her face,
Lingered with me, a sweet, gentle, peaceful space.

Poem -22 - Sweet Memory

Today, I feel different, my heart at peace
Thanks to her sweet smile, and her gentle release
She's pure, innocent, and sweet as can be
A treasure to behold, in her poetic spree
I was bored with life, and its practical ways
But her garden, and poetry, brightened up my days
Luxury, and power, are not everything, I see
There's a void inside, that only love can be
In seven days, I'll leave, and go back to my duty
As an IAS officer, with a life that's not so fruity
I came for investigation, but her garden changed my mind
Now, I'm torn between duty, and this poetic life I find
This profession doesn't allow, for love, or gentle times
I've missed this sweet phase, of life's poetic rhymes
Still, the void remains, a longing to be free
To live a life of poetry, and love, wild, and carefree.

Poem -23 - Three Months Passed Away

Three months have gone by, since that sweet encounter,

The stranger boy, who left, without a further glance or ponder.

No texts, no calls, no words, from him, in all this time,

Yet, I miss him deeply, with a heart that's hard to align.

We met just once, but somehow, he left a mark,

I don't know what happened, or why I feel this spark.

I texted him, "How are you?" after ten long days,

He replied, but I sensed, he'd moved on, in busy ways.

Perhaps he didn't miss me, as I did him, it's clear,

But still, I'll text him once more, and hold back my tear.

Poem – 24 - The Sweetest Call

In celebration, I was lost, yet found,

Missing someone dear, my heart profound.

I texted, "How are you?" and he replied,

"Give me a call, if you're free, I'd love to hear your voice inside."

I called, and words flowed, without a thought,

"You never missed me," I said, my emotions caught.

He replied, with sweetness, "You're dear to me,"

And shared an address, "Come meet me, if you're free."

I was at an award ceremony, but I had to go,

Promising to arrive, within an hour, don't you know.

He said, in a sweet voice, "Come, I'll wait for you,"

My heart skipped a beat, in anticipation, anew.

The address surprised me, a grand office, so fine,

An IAS officer, with a nameplate that shined.

He welcomed me, with a deep smile, so wide,

I asked, "Why hide your identity?" He replied with pride.

"It's part of my profession, dear, a secret to keep,

A visit for official purpose, my identity to reap."

I shared my latest awards, as he attended to his task,
Before leaving, I hugged him tight, our hearts to ask.
"I have to leave," I said, with a heavy heart,
Our time together, a memory to never depart.

Poem – 25 - Deep Feelings

I'm lost in emotions, unsure what's gained or lost,

Longing for someone, my heart forever crossed.

How can I miss him so, when we've just begun?

My feelings swirl, like a storm, yet to be done.

What's happening between us, I'm unsure, yet I feel,

A connection deep, that my heart can't conceal.

He's an officer, a boy of duty and might,

But why do I feel this way, day and endless night?

Oh, God, why am I overwhelmed, unbalanced, and blue?

Why do my emotions rage, like a storm, anew?

I search for answers, but they hide from my sight,

Leaving me with just this feeling, a deep, endless night.

Poem – 26 - Composition in Garden

In every thought of mine, you're always on my mind,

Like a fine wine, your memory is forever intertwined.

Don't you feel the same, don't you feel this way?

My heart sinks deep in thoughts of you, every single day.

I'm lost in what to remember, and what to forget,

No matter how busy I am, my heart still skips a beat.

You're stuck in my heart, like a gentle, sweet refrain,

My feelings soar high, between earth and sky, in vain.

I yearn to see you now, to hold you close and tight,

To hug you every day, and dance beneath the stars' soft light.

Don't you feel the same, don't you feel this way?

My heart beats for you alone, every single day.

Poem – 27 - Pure Feelings

Sitting alone, by the windowpane,

I ponder on sunshine and rain.

Memories of that beautiful day remain,

When someone entered my garden, making it a paradise to gain.

I yearn to hear his voice, so gentle and kind,

Recalling the day we met, with raindrops intertwined.

Do you miss me, as I miss you, with every passing day?

My heart beats with longing, in a loving, melancholic way.

Lying on my bed, I weave love like a thread,

Are you weaving the same, in the silence of your head?

Thinking of you, every day, is my heart's delight,

The most beautiful feeling, that shines with love and light.

Poem - 28 - I Feel You

I'm falling for someone, so sweet and divine,

Falling from the ordinary, into a love so sublime.

He's as sweet as honey, cool as the gentle moon's light,

My music, my melody, my heart's delight.

When I gaze into his eyes, I feel the sunrise high,

When I whisper his name, I feel a fame that touches the sky.

Is it favouritism, or a love game we play?

Only time will tell, but for now, I'll bask in the joy of the day.

Let the moment arrive, when we'll have fun together,

I'll feel happiness overwhelm me, like a gentle, loving weather.

In his presence, I'm submerged in bliss, my heart aglow,

Forever with him, is where I want to go.

Poem - 29 - Asking Questions from Myself

I was a girl who loved myself, content and free,

Why then does someone else appear in my dreams, a mystery to me?

It's true, I often see my favourites in my sleep,

But when he comes, it's different, a feeling I must keep.

I have everything, no void to suffer or grieve,

Yet, why do I miss him particularly, a question I must retrieve?

I'm patient with my feelings, understanding his busy world,

But trying not to think of him hurts, a pain unfurled.

Many people love me, showering me with affection true,

But in my heart, he stays the same, a feeling shining through.

This is the mystery of feelings, why I feel for him so much,

A regret that lingers, a longing that's hard to hush.

I regret because whenever I want him, he's not there,

A bittersweet longing that fills my heart with care.

Poem – 30 - Meeting with Him

Today was the best day, I met him once more,

Ran towards him, leaving city life's din and roar.

I left him behind, but my heart stayed with him true,

Those few minutes we talked, will haunt my dreams anew.

Let me write something good, and complete my new book,

Let me wipe my tears, and change my outlook to look.

But as I met him, I lost myself, it's true,

A strange feeling in my heart, I felt, anew.

I don't know what's in store, for my heart's sake,

Will we be together, or forever apart, I'll wait.

But for now, I'm lost, in the depths of his eyes,

My heart beats for him alone, in sweet, loving surprise.

Poem – 31 - I get touched

I was in my office working with files,

Suddenly that poetic girl's composition made me surprise,

You don't think of me, I think of you every time,

I wish I could tell you that I am not fine.

I miss you a lot, you miss me or not I don't know why?

To console my heart, my very best every time I try.

To treat me like a girl, you are a first boy

Everybody considers me just a beauty toy.

I feel you here, I feel you there, I feel you everywhere,

In times of need, you handle me with such a lovely care.

When I see in your eyes, it seems I am having a drink,

A sudden thought of you makes my heart more sink.

Your sudden touch makes my heart fresh,

When I left your arms, I feel like crash.

It's love or not, I can't make you forget,

I don't know why, to console my heart, my very best every time I try.

Poem - 32 - A Soul So Pure

She seems a deeply emotional soul,

A girl who inhabits her own world,

Creating space for me, free from preconceptions' hold.

Her feelings are remarkably pure and alluring to behold.

Her love confession is genuine and true,

Though she's uncertain about her emotions,

Being a new experience, she's yet to break through.

She claims to be practical, yet a poet at heart,

I found this paradox strange, but chose to remain quiet from the start.

Her poems, however, confess an indirect love for me,

A sentiment she struggles to acknowledge openly.

Despite the challenge, her words reveal a deep affection,

A feeling that, for her, is still hard to comprehend and express with conviction.

Poem – 33 - Her phone call

She called me today, at eve's gentle hush,

I hoped she was fine, as her call lit up my rush.

I answered with a smile, and a heart full of cheer,

"Hello, how are you?" she asked, and I replied, "I'm fine, and I hope you are too, my dear."

She shared her concerns, not of missing me, but of her heart's plight,

I sensed innocence in her words, a vulnerability so bright.

I reassured her, "Of course, I miss you," for she's always on my mind,

A constant presence, a love so hard to define.

She confessed her fears, of emotions that might grow too strong,

Though she tries to console herself each day, her heart still beats with a lovesick song.

I invited her to meet, to bridge the distance between us two,

But she declined, fearing the pain of parting, and the heartache that might ensue.

I'm trapped in her poetic love, in this world that's both cruel and kind,

For I love her too, but reality's harsh grip is hard to unwind.

Poem – 34 - Across the Distance

Three months had passed without a word from her,

Yet memories of her cute texts still lingered, dear.

A single message from her could brighten my day,

And bring a smile to my face, come what may.

I couldn't bear the distance any longer,

So I texted her, "Hello, how are you?"

She replied, "I'm okay, adjusting to this practical world,"

But didn't mention missing me, instead sharing her struggles unfurled.

Her response filled my heart with positive rays,

I confessed, "I missed you, and I'd love to meet you someday."

But she declined, fearing her poetic emotions might create trouble,

Explaining that feelings can be hazardous, becoming obstacles in our life's rubble.

She concluded, "In this practical world, we must adjust,"

Leaving me to ponder, with a heart that still yearned to trust.

Poem – 35 - She Called Again

She called me again, just a few days apart,

Confessing that she still missed me, with a tender heart.

I smiled, and she smiled too, our hearts beating in sync,

In that moment, our connection was rekindled, pure and distinct.

She said, "I want to meet you, but I fear the pain of goodbye,"

"It's impossible to end feelings once they've begun to thrive."

I replied, "Our feelings have already grown strong,

We've become close, unknowingly, our hearts now bound together long."

"Feelings are unconditional," I said, "beyond our control,"

"We have a hold on each other's hearts, a love that makes our spirits whole."

She agreed, "The mystery of our relationship remains to be revealed,"

But accepted my invitation to meet, her feelings now too strong to conceal.

Poem – 36 - She confessed her heart

Struggling the heavy traffic she reached to meet me.

I just hugged her tight and she too closed her eyes.

Seeing her really was like a surprise.

She said, "So really you missed me?"

I replied, "Yes, of course, my sweetheart, don't you?"

She said, "Yeah, that's why I am here."

I said, "You are so adorable and cute; I control my love for you."

She said, "Though I feel a lot for you, but I'm afraid that our bond won't survive in this practical world.

How would we justify this fondness for each other?

I can't bear it if my emotions suffer."

That's why I'm afraid to meet you frequently.

What if my feelings grew so high with time?

I said, "Feelings once grown can't be suppressed."

She said, "Yes, when I get apart from you, I get depressed.

I get apart physically, but you are constant in my mind."

I said, "It means our souls matched from inside vibes."

She said, "I do believe in getting a soulmate instead of a husband.

Because who guarantees that marriage will last the same?

It is based on duties and obligations, yet fades with time.

But a bond of soulmates remains intact throughout life."

I am afraid to marry someone because if he left me, what would I do?

To accept someone in any way, for me, strong love is the first rule.

Her words mesmerized me a lot.

She touched my heart at one shot.

I asked, "So you never thought to marry someone?"

She said, "No, because the generation of my age only knows lust.

Innocent girls are used as products for bed.

After fulfilling a few days' passion, they move to the next.

I can't share myself with anyone so easily, unless my soul completely meets.

I can remain with myself instead of a risky bond.

In the 21st-century world, true love is actually no more."

Poem - 37 - Time Flew Away

Time flew away on wings, our moments lost in air,

I said, "We'll talk again soon, and share our time with care."

But duty called, I had to leave for work's sake,

She whispered, "I hate this practical world, it's a heartache."

"I just want to compose, to create and be loved,"

She said, her voice a melody, sent from above.

I replied, "Alright, my sleeping beauty, compose your heart's song,

I'll love you always, and keep you safe, all life long."

She said, "I don't know if it's love, but we're more than friends,

You're my soulmate, a feeling that transcends."

A bond beyond words, a connection of the heart,

A love that's hard to define, yet never departs.

She understood the demands of my bureaucratic life,

A world of duties, where love's a rare, precious strife.

I said, "You're right, my sweetheart, it's a challenging road,"

She whispered, "Take care of yourself, as you depart, my love."

Poem – 38 - I Missed Him Suddenly

In the still of midnight, I felt a sudden pang,

A longing for him, so strong, it made my heart sang.

I reached for my phone, and dialled his number fast,

He answered, "Yes, how are you?" but before I could speak at last.

He said, "I love you," and my heart skipped a beat,

I froze, unable to respond, my words stuck in my throat so neat.

He urged, "You say it too," and to my surprise, I replied,

"I love you," without a thought, my heart spoke, and my words collided.

I couldn't grasp this love-like game, so new and so true,

I confessed, "I've never said this to anyone, but I said it to you."

He smiled, and said, "Take care, and sleep tight,"

And in that moment, I realized my feelings shone with equal light.

Poem – 39 - Funny Conversation

I rang him up and said with a grin,

"I want to learn discipline from you, to fit into your officer's skin."

He laughed and said, "First, you must leave your sleeping beauty zone,

For half your day is lost in sleep, and tasks are left undone, unknown."

He advised, "With your poetic heart, you must be career-oriented too,

For money doesn't grow on trees, it's earned, and that's what you must pursue."

I agreed, "From today, I'll study hard, and give my books a new face,

No longer tired and resting in my almirah, a forgotten, dusty place."

I shared, "I've nominated myself for a literary prize, though I'm unsure of the test,

But I'll work hard every day, and do my best."

He encouraged, "Don't worry, one day you'll win the Booker, you'll see,

I said, My favourite teacher always wished it for me and it will be."

He reminded, "My sleeping beauty, your sleep destroys your day,

So rise and shine, and chase your dreams, come what may."

Poem - 40 - I Am Trying to Be Disciplined

I'm trying to be disciplined, to work hard every day,

To make a fresh start, and drive my dreams on the way.

I must prepare for competitive exams, and be at my best,

But I'll also nurture my poetic charm, and let my creativity rest.

I'll believe in myself, and when stress takes its toll,

I'll talk to my soulmate, who makes my heart and spirit whole.

He boosts my confidence, and helps me shine so bright,

With his love and support, everything feels just right.

It's time to work hard, and make my dreams unfold,

The practical world is challenging, but love makes life worth more than gold.

With care and affection, life can be refreshing and new,

A chance to start anew, and make my heart and spirit renew.

Oh God, once again I'm missing him, feeling his absence so true,

But I'll stay focused, and work towards my goals, with his love shining through.

Poem – 41 - His Words Heal Me

I sit amidst chaos, in my room's confront zone,

Books scattered, pens astray, yet my heart feels at home.

The sweet scent of perfumes envelops my bed,

Fresh flowers surround me, calming my restless head.

Though wishes pour in from loved ones, dear and true,

His words overshadow all, a balm to my soul anew.

"Believe in yourself and your work," he says with gentle might,

"Keep smiling, no matter life's plight."

"You will forever be in my heart," he whispers low and sweet,

"Whenever you need me, I'll be there to greet.

With you, my heart beats alone, my love I'll only share,

Your soul and heart, so pure, beyond compare."

Poem - 42 - Success at Exam

Today, I cleared the revenue officer exam with flying colours bright,

A first step towards success, a milestone in sight.

Everyone praised me with love and warm regards,

But one thing remained, a secret to be shared.

This success needed celebration, a joy to unfold,

A secret to be whispered to my love, my officer boy to hold.

To my surprise, he called me, congratulations flowing free,

With lots of love, he spoke, and my heart felt ecstasy.

He wanted to meet me soon, to share in my delight,

I too decided to meet him, to bask in love's warm light.

In this moment, success felt sweeter, with love by my side,

A celebration to cherish, a memory to abide.

Poem - 43 - The Most Beautiful Moment

In a lush garden, he arrived, a sight to behold,

I ran to him, and hugged him tight, my heart full of gold.

I thanked him for teaching me discipline's gentle art,

And for caring for me like a delicate flower, a tender heart.

He said, "More colours of success are needed to paint this life,

Bring change to people's lives through the service you provide, and thrive."

"You're great at spreading love," he said with a smile so bright,

"You've made a place in my heart, in just a few meetings, a precious sight."

He asked, "Promise me you'll always love me, and greet me the same,"

I vowed, "I promise, my soulmate, forever and always, I'll remain."

In that moment, our hearts entwined, a love so pure and true,

A promise sealed, a bond strengthened, forever shining through.

Poem – 44 - Two Years Gone

Two years have passed, a balancing act I've played,

Between my poetic life and professional way.

A Booker nomination, a surprise to behold,

A dream within reach, my heart doth unfold.

Yet, in these busy years, I've missed my soulmate's face,

Our connections limited to two brief, distant calls in space.

My heart yearns to talk to my teacher, mentor, and friend,

My beyond favourite guide, who helped my spirit ascend.

Without her teachings, I'd have never made it through,

Her wisdom and love, a beacon shining bright and true.

Life's preciousness I've come to know, through love's pure light,

A treasure to cherish, a gift that makes my heart take flight.

Let's see what's next, as life unfolds its mysterious way,

A new chapter awaits, with hope, love, and a brighter day.

Poem – 45 - I Got the Booker Prize

Today was overwhelming, a dream come true,
I was selected for the Booker Prize, my heart anew.
Family members praised me, hugged me tight,
My favourite teacher's dream had finally taken flight.
I took the prize with him on stage, a promise fulfilled,
A vow made in my writing days, my heart's will.
This moment satisfied my soul, made everyone proud,
The poetess's success shone bright, a joyous crowd.
My soulmate, my officer boy, beamed with joy for me,
I invited him to spend a few days, a celebration to be.
Together we'll bask in this glory, a love that's strong and true,
A moment to treasure, a memory to forever shine through.

Poem – 46 - After Six Months

He came after six months, a long-awaited sight,

I teased, "You completely forgot me, out of sight."

He replied, "Office work and professional life kept me tied,

But now, with time on my hands, I've come to be with you, side by side."

He said, "This beautiful vacation, I'll spend only with you,

I too get bored with practical life, and need poetic love anew."

I hugged him tight, welcoming him with a grin,

We talked, laughed, and shared our emotions, our hearts entwined within.

The whole night, we conversed, our love shining bright and true,

A reunion of hearts, a love that forever shines through.

Poem – 47 - I Sang for Him

The moon shines bright, and I smile with glee,
My head on his lap, a tender intimacy.
He kisses my forehead with lips so soft and kind,
I smile, but don't reply with a kiss, my heart entwined.
He rests his head on my shoulder, holding me tight,
I decide to sing for him, through the silent night.
He yearns to listen, with love that overflows,
Seeking comfort and peace, as my melodies unfold.
I promise that my lyrics will captivate his soul,
Freezing time, as our love becomes the heart's goal.
With every note, our bond will strengthen and grow,
In this serenade, our love will forever glow.

Poem – 48 - You Are Saved in My Eyes

Your face is etched in my mind, a constant sight,

I see you everywhere, a vision that's always in light.

I meet many, but none compare to you,

My heart skips a beat when I recall your name, anew.

Sleep eludes me, and my day begins,

Though surrounded by people, I feel alone, and you're nowhere to be seen.

Your photographs are treasured between my books,

Fragrant perfumes scent the pages, a sensory hook.

Many love me, but our bond is the strongest tie,

You're the title in my life's syllabus, without you, I'd ask why.

No matter who comes and goes, my love for you will remain,

Forever and always, in a special way, reserved for you, my heart's refrain.

In your arms, I find complete love, nothing more I need,

You're saved in my eyes, forever, my heart you've freed.

You stole my heart, and it's yours to keep,

Forever and always, my love, in eternal sleep.

Poem – 49 - Don't You Feel It's Tough to Love You

Don't you feel it's tough to love you,

To hug you hard, then leave you, too?

Don't you feel it's tough to miss you so,

To kiss you softly, then let you go?

Don't you feel it's tough to hold your hand,

Feeling the warmth, then leaving the land?

Don't you feel it's tough to drown in your eyes,

Waiting for you, with a heart that sighs?

The longing and the leaving, a bittersweet refrain,

A love that's strong, yet painful, like summer rain.

The memories linger, a tender, loving ache,

A heart that beats for you, though we're apart, for now, my love, my heart.

Poem – 50 - The Soulful Kiss

My dearest love, you're made to be loved, as your name implies,

A love that's different, beyond the ordinary skies.

Being apart from you is beyond my control,

But life demands many roles, and our love must unfold.

We're lucky to have found each other, connected soul to soul,

You once said, as a poet, I had no heart to make whole.

But I gave you your wandering heart, where love resides,

And with trust, our bond abides.

After fulfilling our duties, we'll love hard when we meet,

Together in times of need, our love will forever repeat.

You're safe in my arms, and life is lucky to give love by chance.

He held me close, hugged me tight, and I felt complete,

Free from worldly bonds, our love transcends, a love so unique.

Love's not just bodily needs, but a bond that never dies,

Beyond love exists between you and I, a love that touches the skies.

He kissed my lips, and I smiled, wondering if I should take it otherwise,

But he said, in deep love, a little romance is justified, and I realized.

I smiled, and said, this little romance is enough for me,

For true love, such expressions are justified, wild, and carefree.

We hugged each other tight, and I closed my eyes,

Love gets love, a surprise that touches the heart, and never dies.

About the Author

Priya Singh

Miss Priya Singh, a 23-year-old multifaceted and acclaimed poet, lyricist, screenwriter, and novelist who has been making waves in the literary world with her exceptional talent and dedication. Born in Meerut, India, into a family of professors, Priya's love for literature and learning was nurtured from a young age. A medalist in MA English Literature, Priya's impressive educational background has been a testament to her passion for the written word.

Priya's literary journey has been marked by numerous milestones, including the international success of her song "The Snowfall of December", which was produced in the UK and became a national sensation in India. Her books, such as "I Found My Love", "Between You & I", and "My Teacher, My Lifeline", have been bestsellers and have received critical acclaim globally. To date, Priya has penned 10 poignant poetic fictions that have captivated readers with their unique blend of romance, introspection, and emotional depth.

A recipient of numerous prestigious awards, Priya has been recognized for her outstanding contributions to literature. Some of her notable awards include the International Poetry Digest Award (USA), the Elite Writers Status Award, and the Eminence Excellence Award (Dubai). Her book ""My Teacher, My Lifeline"" won the coveted Best Fiction Book of the Year Award, a testament to her exceptional storytelling skills. She has also been honored with the title of Youngest Poet of the Year (Bangkok) and has received the Green Education Excellence Award.

Priya's work has been appreciated by dignitaries and literary luminaries alike, including Prime Minister Narendra Modi, Her Excellency Anandi Ben Patel, and other esteemed personalities. Her writings have been featured in various international magazines, and she has represented India globally with her poetry, inspiring audiences with her message of peace, love, and motivation.

As a sought-after guest and keynote speaker, Priya has been invited to various eminent universities and poetic events, where she has shared her insights and expertise with students, scholars, and poetry enthusiasts. Her presence has been a source of inspiration, and her words have left a lasting impact on all who have had the privilege of listening to her.

With her impressive body of work, Priya has established herself as a leading literary voice, and her writings continue to captivate audiences worldwide.

www.ingramcontent.com/pod-product-compliance
Lightning Source LLC
LaVergne TN
LVHW041547070526
838199LV00046B/1860